BECAUSE OF YOU,
Dad

© 2019 Deseret Book Company

Illustrations © 2019 Kevin Keele

All rights reserved. No part of this book may be reproduced in any form or by any means without permission in writing from the publisher, Deseret Book Company, at permissions@deseretbook.com or PO Box 30178, Salt Lake City, Utah 84130. This work is not an official publication of The Church of Jesus Christ of Latter-day Saints. The views expressed herein are the responsibility of the author and do not necessarily represent the position of the Church or of Deseret Book Company.

DESERET BOOK is a registered trademark of Deseret Book Company.

Visit us at deseretbook.com

Library of Congress Cataloging-in-Publication Data
Names: Keele, Kevin, illustrator.
Title: Because of you, Dad / illustrated by Kevin Keele.
Description: Salt Lake City, Utah : Deseret Book, [2019] | Summary: "A children's picture book expressing appreciation for fathers"–Provided by publisher.
Identifiers: LCCN 2018039965 | ISBN 9781629725611 (hardbound : alk. paper)
Subjects: | CYAC: Father and child—Fiction. | Mormons—Fiction. | LCGFT: Picture books.
Classification: LCC PZ7.1.K398 Be 2019 | DDC [E]—dc23
LC record available at https://lccn.loc.gov/2018039965

Printed in China
RR Donnelley, Shenzhen, China   11/2018

10   9   8   7   6   5   4   3   2   1

BECAUSE OF YOU,
Dad

Illustrated by KEVIN KEELE

DESERET BOOK

BECAUSE OF YOU, DAD,
*I feel ten feet tall,
like I can tackle anything.*

{ And I know I have SHOULDERS TO RIDE ON when I get tired. }

I know what and who I WANT TO BE when I grow up—or at least grow older.

I believe I CAN DO ANYTHING, and I know I'll always have someone else who believes it too.

Because of you, Dad, I know the BEST STORIES
...that are mostly true.

I AM ALWAYS LAUGHING

(or rolling my eyes at the world's corniest jokes).

I know the meaning of ADVENTURE.

And I LOVE THE AMAZING WORLD around me (even when the world is just our backyard).

I know HOW to HAVE FUN
(and do donuts in the parking lot).

But I also understand the IMPORTANCE of HARD WORK.

And that it's a good thing to CHASE MY DREAMS.

Because of you, Dad, I know more about my FATHER IN HEAVEN.

And what unfailing love looks like—and feels like.

I have a TESTIMONY of PRIESTHOOD power and how it can be used to do the Lord's work.

And I recognize that making time to LOVE and SERVE others can make all the difference in the world.

Because of you, Dad, I know that
WINNING ISN'T EVERYTHING.

And that sometimes losing means even more.

I know WHERE TO TURN for help with life's toughest problems.

And I believe Heavenly Father
HEARS AND ANSWERS MY PRAYERS—even when I don't
recognize the answers right away.

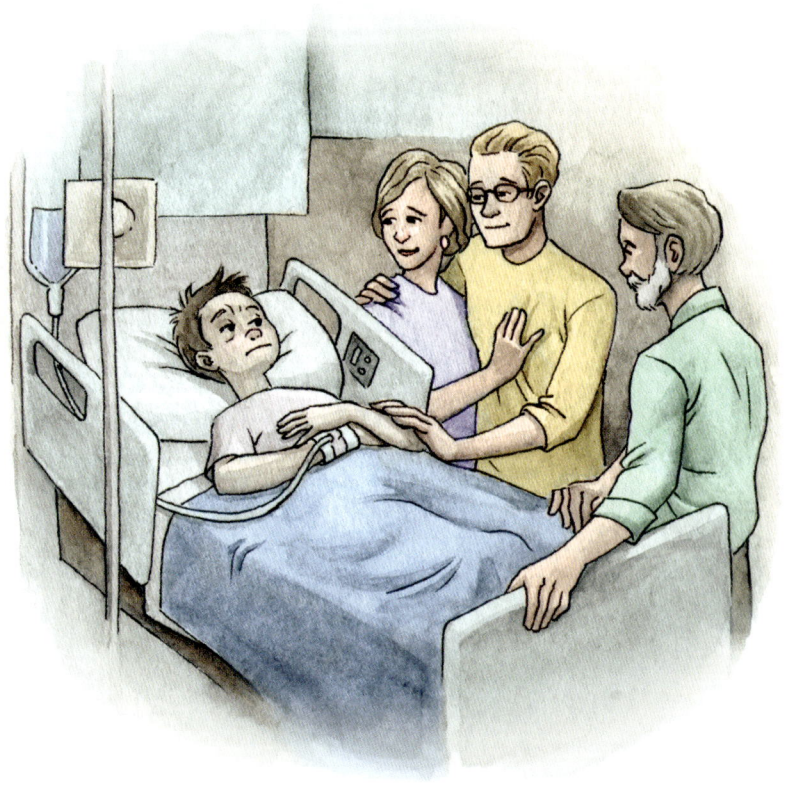

Because of you, Dad, I know I always have
A HOME TO GO TO, no matter what happens.

✳ And I know how to BE THE BEST ME I can be. ✳

I have the best TEACHER—
and the best FRIEND—in the world.

Dad—can you see it?
Because of you, I HAVE EVERYTHING I really need.

So, thank you, Dad. It's all BECAUSE OF YOU.

Because of you, Dad...